M SUBRAMANIAM AND ANR. V. S JANAKI AND ANR.

VOLUME 2, ISSUE 1 OF BRILLOPEDA

MEHER MANSI

Copyright © Meher Mansi
All Rights Reserved.

This book has been published with all efforts taken to make the material error-free after the consent of the author. However, the author and the publisher do not assume and hereby disclaim any liability to any party for any loss, damage, or disruption caused by errors or omissions, whether such errors or omissions result from negligence, accident, or any other cause.

While every effort has been made to avoid any mistake or omission, this publication is being sold on the condition and understanding that neither the author nor the publishers or printers would be liable in any manner to any person by reason of any mistake or omission in this publication or for any action taken or omitted to be taken or advice rendered or accepted on the basis of this work. For any defect in printing or binding the publishers will be liable only to replace the defective copy by another copy of this work then available.

Contents

Preface

"Start writing, no matter what. The water does not flow until the faucet is turned on".

-Louis L'Amour

Hundreds of students and professors are contributing their work to Brillopedia, we are here to provide ample information about Law and Contemporary issues. Our aim is to provide a platform for today's generation to express their views and ideas on law and contemporary law.

Publication

This research paper is published in volume 2, issue 1 of Brillopedia

CHAPTER ONE

ABSTRACT

Everyone hopes for a crimeless society. But it is nearly impossible, which is why there are codes and legislative instruments to punish it and guarantee protectionto the public. Indian law regarding criminal matters goes way backto the British period. The most important code Indian Penal Code (IPC), 1860 was a British legislation. The other corroborating procedural laws were also introduced in the British era but were repealed and amended accordingly for the evolving nature of crimes. India follows the deterrent theory in punishing crimes and it has worked well with some implementation lacunae. Criminal law occupies a predominant place in the agencies of social control. It is a mechanism forged by the states to deal with anti-social behavior. Criminal procedure code (CrPC) forms the foundations for dealing with crimes in the country. The CrPC is an inseparable part of penal law in the country and the effectiveness of IPC depends on the proper implementation of this procedural law. Criminal law of any society or state is described as the true mirror of that society as it reflects all the fundamental values of the society. So the provisions which provide for investigation, fair trial, speedy and full trial are the cornerstones of the society's treatment of the criminals and in turn affect the standing of the society. Formerly in the British Era there were very few courts to deal with criminal matters, but now the apex court is also vested with power to deal with the criminal cases. The cases over the years grew and contributed to judicial activism and shaped the criminal law regime. This is one such landmark judgements which gave clarity on the technicalities of the subject.

Case Study on M Subramaniam and Anr. v. S Janaki and Anr. (2020) 16 SCC 728- Before the Supreme Court Decided by a three judge bench comprising of N.V.Ramana, Mohan M.S. and SanjivKhanna, JJ.

CHAPTER TWO

FACTS

The present case is a criminal appeal to the Supreme Court filed under article 136 of the Indian Constitution. The respondent in the present cases is a one of the trustees of ADS educational trust. The ADS educational trust was established in 1985 for the purpose of furthering quality education and promoting it. In promotion of their objectivethe trust set up Sri Angalamman College of Engineering and Technology at Trichy in 1987. The appellants in the present case are the Chairman and Vice-chairman of the college respectively. The respondent filed a case in 2008 where she directed the police to register anFirst Information Report (FIR) against them and file the final report in accordance with law. In the 2008 case filed by the respondent, the appellants were not even recognized as parties. Aggrieved by this, the appellants approached this court for relief. The appellants claim that the respondent does not have locus standi to file the criminal case. The criminal case is just an attempt to wreak havoc and vengeance in a civil dispute which was pending. The appellants also claim that the first respondent was removed from service due on account of fraud and forgery. The present case challenges the cases filed and FIR registered as per the order given by the High court of Madras. The police proceeded the investigation despite the stay order given by the present court. The Madras High Court's order was produced before the Supreme Court. If the Supreme Court rejects this special leave petition the police would continue the investigation and conclude it with a charge sheet or final closure report. Therefore the apex court ordered that the police should not proceed with the investigation till the judgement is given in the present special leave petition.

ISSUES

- Whether a complainant can approach the High Court, for a remedy, if FIR not registered under Section 154 of Criminal Procedure Code (CrPC)?
- What is the scope of powers of Magistrate undersection 156(3)?

CHAPTER THREE

RULE OF LAW

- If a person's complaint is not being registered by the police and no FIR is registered under section 154 of CrPC then he can approach the Superintendent of Police under section 154(3), if still aggrieved can file an application to the Magistrate under section 156(3).[1] The learned Magistrate has all the powers to direct to register the FIR and proceed with the investigation. The provision also authorises the magistrate to monitor the investigation if needed. Section 156(3) gives very extensive powers to the Magistrate even upto the extent where police fall back in the investigation, the magistrate can interfere and direct the police to investigate properly and fulfill their responsibilities.

- If the person is aggrieved that an FIR is not registered or the investigation is not properly conducted, then they cannot go to the High Court under article 226 of the Constitution or cannot file a writ petition. They should approach the Magistrate under section 156(3) of CrPC, if the FIR is already registered the Magistrate can direct proper investigation to be conducted. The magistrate can even go to the extent of replacing the investigating officer for the purpose of proper investigation to be conducted at the magistrate's discretion.[2]

[1]SakiriVasu v. State Of Uttar Pradesh And Others, (2008) 2 SCC 409.

[2]Id.; State of Bihar v. J.A.C. Saldanha, (1980) 1 SCC 544; SudhirBhaskarraoTambe v. HemantYashwantDhage and Others, (2016) 6 SCC 277.

CHAPTER FOUR

JUDGMENT

The court held that he magistrate has the power to deal with any grievances regarding FIR. The court set aside the order of the High Court. The court further added that civil dispute should not be given the colour of criminal offence and the mere existence of civil case cannot justify not registering FIR.[1]

[1]M Subramaniam and Anr. v. S Janaki and Anr. (2020) 16 SCC 72.

CHAPTER FIVE

ANALYSIS

The present case is a land mark judgement. FIR is the foundation and bedrock for any investigation. It is the first step of a trial. That goes wrong and everything goes downhill. Therefore it is very important to provide for accurate guidelines to direct the police and other officials involved for a proper trial. The stakeholders in a criminal case have a lot at stake. As the experts and many judges say thousands of culprits can escape but not even one innocent should be punished. Therefore the trial and investigation procedure of a crime should be accurately done and should be appropriate to the last detail. The accuracy should be proven beyond reasonable doubt only then there is fair trial. Chapter 12 of the CrPC is a very important chapter in furtherance of fair trial. Chapter 12 provides for the information to the police and their powers to investigate. That is regarding the FIR and their power to investigate. One of the important parts of the provision is the conflict between the courts and the authorities. The courts might be overpowered even to the extent of completely taking the authority to replace investigating officers. The court can take any measure at its discretion. The courts are given a huge responsibility through the provisions of the chapter 12. The importance of the case can be seen through the object and intention behind chapter 12. This case furthers that standing of law and substantiates it more.

Object of chapter 12: the object of chapter 12 is to have a fast and fair investigation. Section 154-176 provide for the speedy justice by giving accurate measures to be taken when someone approaches the police authorities. The police in the country are infamous for friendly policing. But the legal provisions give the highest responsibility and they should be one of the strongest links between the state and people. The chapter provides for very elaborate provisions to deal with investigations. The sections are drafted in a way to provide for a recorded offence to help in the trial and investigation. The reported offence then will be investigated and dealt within the limits of the law, devoid of arbitrariness. The right to fair trial is right guaranteed under article 21 of the Constitution to every person, so every accused is entitled to right to fair investigation. The Court also held in a case concerning chapter 12 of CrPC, that it is the duty of the court to accept and accord its approval only to a report which is the result of faithful and fruitful investigation. Chapter 12 of the CrPC is also important in the sense that it differentiates between cognizable and non-cognizable offences. By doing so it gives power to the Magistrate to enjoin in cases of non-cognizable offences. All these details and guidelines are highlighted in the given case.

Judiciary v. police: one of the most noteworthy parts of this case is the balance of relationship between the judiciary and the police. The remedy for not registering an FIR is to approach the judiciary, in this case the magistrate. The statutory remedies are given under three sections- 154(3) provides to approach the SP, if not satisfied then to the Judicial Magistrate under section 156(3) r/w 190 and the last one is section 200 which gives the similar status as non cognizable case where the magistrate takes cognizance. Over the years the judiciary's powers were considered overlapping and they were restricted. In many cases the courts regarded that the subordinate courts do not have inherent powers and cannot transgress their limits. But now, the plethora of cases available on the issues of FIR registration have changed this standing of law. The subordinate courts have all the incidental power to interfere with the investigation if it is not done properly. The section 156(3) gives wide powers to the judiciary to deal with the cases of FIR. It includes all such incidental powers required to ensure a proper investigation. Nevertheless, both the bodies are independent and exercise the granted powers in their realm, subject to the rights of the court to intervene. The functions of both the bodies are not overlapping but complementary to each other.[1] The magistrates are kept posted about the case at each level of investigation, if there is any problem the magistrate may interfere on their own discretion.

[1]King Emperor v. KhwajaNazir Ahmad (AIR 1945 PC 18).

CHAPTER SIX

PRECEDENTS

The Apex Court has decided on the issues regarding FIRs and the remedies available many times over the years. Some of the pertinent cases which establish the law for this case are:

- Mohd. Yousuf v. AfaqJahan and Ors.[1]: The court held that the magistrate can take cognizance and order investigation under 156(3). Magistrate can direct the police to file the FIR for beginning the investigation. It is not illegal to do so.

- Dilawar Singh v. State of Delhi[2]: the court reiterated the same standing as in the Yousuf case, it said that the magistrate can monitor and direct even after the FIR is filed and the investigation has begun. When aggrieved person not satisfied he can approach the court. The court can order proper investigation measures as fit.
- State of Bihar and Ors. v. J.A.C. Saldanha and Ors.[3]: the court held that the magistrate can reopen the investigation even after the police submits the final report.
- SudhirBhaskarraoTambe v. HemantYashwantDhage and Ors.[4]: the court held the same thing as in Sakiri's[5] case when there is a conflict regarding FIR, the remedy is not to approach the High Court rather approach the Magistrate under 156(3).

On the whole the present case summarized all the above mentioned ratios. The judgement and decision was relied on the landmark Sakiri case. This case reiterated the power of magistrate court under section 156(3) and added that when an act confers jurisdiction all such incidental powers to employ the means are vested with the same. Likewise in the present case all the means to conduct proper investigation are also granted to the magistrate. Therefore the order of the High court was set aside.

[1](2006) 1 SCC 627.
[2](2007) 12 SCC 641.
[3](1980) 1 SCC 554.
[4](2016) 6 SCC 277.
[5]*Supra* note 1.

CHAPTER SEVEN

CONCLUSION

The underpinning of the case is the jurisdiction of the High court and the subordinate courts. The underlying issue of the case highlights the importance of FIR and the remedies if FIR not registered. It highlights that a timely FIR with possible details might help build a strong case for prosecution and direct the investigation. Without the filing of the FIR there might be dereliction of duty of the police. The court substantiates all the previous precedent sand gives clarity as to when the judicial remedy of writ petition should be taken up. The court clarifies that it can only be taken after exhaustion of all the statutory remedies under CrPC. The high courts are already burdened with many cases, the alternative remedies should be exhausted before reaching the high court. Approaching the High court will delay the investigation and overburden the High Court and result in dismissal outrightly. The Magistrates are set up for fast and just trial and investigation. The case clearly signifies the chronological remedies available. The exhaustion of the remedies should be done in a chronological and cautious manner within the existing legal regime.